arguments with gravity

New Canadian Poets Series

This series of titles from Quarry Press charts new directions being taken in contemporary Canadian poetry by presenting the first book-length work of innovative writers.

Other titles in the series include *Undressing the Dark* by Barbara Carey, *The Big Life Painting* by Ron Charach, *Stalin's Carnival* by Steven Heighton, *The Speed of the Wheel Is Up to the Potter* by Sandy Shreve, *The Untidy Bride* by Sandra Nicholls, *Mating in Captivity* by Genni Gunn, *Why Is Snow So White?* by F.H. LowBeer, *The River and The Lake* by Joanne Page, *The Slow Reign of Calamity Jane* by Gillian Robinson, and *I Mention the Garden for Clarity* by Vivian Marple.

arguments with gravity

by Michael Crummey

For Caroline,

Hope you enjoy some of these!

All the best,

Michael Crummey

QUARRY PRESS

The publisher acknowledges the support of The Canada Council, Ontario Arts Council, and Department of Canadian Heritage.

Canadian Cataloguing in Publication Data

Crummey, Michael, 1965
  Arguments with gravity

(New Canadian poets series)
ISBN 1-55082-171-7

  I. Title II. Series

PS8555.R84.A98 1996   C811'.54   C96-900669-1
PR9199.3.C718A98 1996

Cover art entitled "Leaving The Farm" by Don Maynard, reproduced with the artist's permission.
Design by Susan Hannah.

Printed in Canada by AGMV I'imprimiere Inc., Cap-Saint-Ignace, Quebec.

Published by Quarry Press, Inc., P.O. Box 1061, Kingston, Ontario K7L 4Y5.

Published in the United Kingdom for Cardiff Academic Press.

Contents

The Air Around Their Bodies

One of The Lives I Have Not Lived

Part of It

Redefining The Kiss

The River You Remember

*There's nothing human that isn't betrayed
and I know nothing but what's human.*
Patrick Friesen

for Mom and Dad

THE AIR AROUND
THEIR BODIES

*But walking along, the body is weighted
a little to the left. It has that
imperceptible limp.*

Roo Borson

Apprenticeships

How everything begins with technique
with simple repetition
the way the old masters learned
the human form by sketching it in charcoal
drawing and redrawing the hand,
the cord of muscles in the shoulder,
the thighs, the hair at the back of the neck,
until the air around the body is
luminous with the body's history,
its intent

By the age of twelve my father
could clean a fish in fifteen seconds
the gutting knife tracing the cod's spine
beneath the scaly flesh,
his blind fingers working beside the blade
pulling the back-bone clear with
the wet web of fish guts,
twelve hours a stretch he was at it some days

A hundred times now I've traced
that life and still I have not
set down what makes it important,
how little I knew of the man who
made me, who held me as a child,
the tools he started out with
his long apprenticeship

Something too obvious to be said simply
refuses to rise to the light of the words,
something as ordinary, as perfectly
proportioned as my father's hands
growing old

~

Why Men Play Hockey

A True Story

Lunar eclipse over southern Ontario:
It's cold and cloudless, December
the planets perfectly rehearsed,
earth's shadow cast against the night sky
like the outline of a hand projected
onto a screen,
the white stone of the moon travelling
through a tide of darkness

A friend and her teenage daughters
are triangled in a backyard where
the diminishing blue light sifts
through the branches of bare trees;
they are wrapped in scarves and thick coats,
their breath the colour of surf
in the night air, lunar, phosphorescent
the heat of their bodies strung to
the pull of the moon

It's that gravity,
how they are cradled by it
like electrons circling the nucleus of an atom —
how they hold their places as the planets align
and the tide cycles through them,
the first dark crescent of blood
descending with the new light,
their periods coming one after the other then
as the moon moves clear
into the night sky

~

Three Pictures of Ann

I

The blade of her right shoulder
a blue tattoo;
back still wet from a shower
the skin studded with
tiny beads of water

Twenty-four
she doesn't believe in God or in love
towels her damp hair
into tangles

Blue scar stitched beneath skin
where it can't be reached
fixed there
almost permanent

II

White duvet
the warmth of her asleep
the fact that she
doesn't need you to be here

She trusts herself implicitly
the way a sleeper trusts the heart
to continue on its own,
as if her body is
everything there is to know;
pierced her ears with a sewing needle
a bar of soap held behind
each lobe in turn

A single light turned to the wall
on her desk, blur of her face almost
touching your face;
silver earrings
hoops the size of an iris

III

All week in the lab
she dissects small animals
opening the tiny cavity of their chests
to study the cardio-vascular systems,
the gastro-intestinal tracts,
setting their bodies to memory

At breakfast now,
newspaper opened like a specimen on the table
a long gray braid of smoke
curling above her head

Ask her sometime,
she can tell you why
nothing lasts forever

Looks up from the paper,
eyes so dark they seem
to have no pupil,
a cigarette held halfway
to her mouth

What, she says to you
What is it?

~

Near Jack's Pond Park

The water is placid
    ego-less
    the perfect contemplation of the surface
mirrors blue sky
a stand of spruce trees on the shore

A single loon moves toward
    the water's centre
    a fluid ripple-less motion —
only the bird's voice
makes it real

Diving, it disappears into
    its own reflection
    into the silence of the water's forest
the strange depth of the dark boughs
waving below the surface

~

Where The Words Come From

Sometimes it's as simple as Lorna Crozier
on the back cover of *The Garden Going
On Without Us*, the smile that confirms
she's a woman who likes her pleasure
the thick curls of hair you can imagine
a hand getting lost in;
or Bronwen Wallace in her last book
her head turned toward the camera
with an expression you can't quite place
a look that says she's told you everything
she's able to tell now

There's the picture of Pat Lowther in *15 Canadian Poets*
the frizz of her shoulder-length hair
tied back with a kerchief,
the beautiful slightly-skewed length of her face
that suggests a kind of wisdom or sorrow
something rooted in the violence we visit
on one another, how it shapes us;
her lips parted just enough to show
the white enamel of teeth, those small stones

The *blue* photograph of Jeni Couzyn, her *Selected Poems*
the symmetrical oval of her face which is mostly light
the blue-black darkness of the hair parted
above the forehead and combed straight to her shoulders
her eyes staring through the filtered blue light
as if she were looking into the camera
from beneath the ocean's surface;
her features are soft and barely focused
they are filled with a grace that has known
butchery and swallowed it, drowned it in
the gentleness of a face that is mostly light
tinged with blue

~

News From Home: Metamorphosis

The most extraordinary things touch the lives
of the people closest to me
                       events that move in them
like a new heart
change them in ways I can only guess at —

A military pilot misplacing the blue of the sky
on a barrel roll
                   plane accelerating into the ground
where the debris scatters across miles of tundra
one body burnt and lying clear in a shallow pool
                          of water
the second in pieces among the wreckage
My brother first on the scene
searching for a leg, a hand, the head
       aware of how everything he is moves in his skin
like water in a flask
of the way his shoulders turn and roll in their sockets
as he bends to lift a shard of metal
of the silence with which his body
goes about its business
as if it were something separate from him
a stranger

Mom on shift in Emergency the night
three young people are brought in DOA
            a winter accident on the road to Quebec
my children, she is thinking
she is covering each body with a white sheet
the bloody clothes
            the disfigured faces
she is thinking how helpless she is

She has memories of me cocooned inside her
a stranger to her then
                changing her body's shape
its rhythms
its needs
        remembers how she craved ice cream all through
                                the pregnancy

What she wants now is more complicated
she wants it to stop snowing outside
she wants to turn her back on this room for good
and can't

You can hear the difference in their voices when they call
how they have grown away from and toward me all at once
and I am changed too by this news from home
by the slow metamorphosis of the people I love;
together we are becoming something we barely recognize
something more fragile
                something tougher than we imagined possible

~

Delayed

His mother had sent him across the road
for milk or bread, or some other necessity,
he pushed on his father's over-sized shoes
and the driver of the Coca Cola truck
didn't see him when he fell beneath the wheels,
only felt the boy's presence there, the fragile skull
collapsing like a small unimportant star.

I had been sent for milk as well —
a tarp thrown over the accident by then,
the corners held by cases of Cola,
and some of what the boy had been
spilled into the open air on the pavement,
as if still trying to make its way home.
A small town crowd had gathered and
his brother was there, crying on
the wooden steps of the store —
older than me, and someone
I had learned to be afraid of,
a fighter, cruel and stupidly fearless,
his twelve year old knuckles
white with scars.
I felt sorry for him then, seeing
what he had lost, watching his body shake
with sobs, as if a man's fist held his shirt
and would not let go.

In the end I went inside to buy the milk,
feeling ridiculous with my handful of coins
and then the wet carton under my arm;
a circle of people surrounded
the yellow rustle of tarp
as if they expected a miracle,
but my mother was waiting at home
and I could not stay.

I climbed the hill toward our street,
the weight of something huge and wordless
in my step; I was late arriving that afternoon
and couldn't properly explain
why I was delayed, and don't expect
I've properly explained it now

∼

Northern Ontario: Finnish Cemetery

Mortared stone at the entrance,
the rows of unbordered gravesites
bordered by a narrow band of spruce.
In the wilt of afternoon heat
her father walks ahead with the mower,
his long complicated silence buried in
the sloppy growl of the engine
while she follows behind, holding a scythe,
taking down the waist-high purple
of lupins around her grandfather's grave.

Foreign names chiselled into marble,
words the country has never learned
to properly speak —
Koivula, Korhonen, Koski —
this century's immigrants, arriving
to clear a piece of land with an axe
and the strength of a body that knows
it can't go home.
Some giving up hope in the end,
broken by root-infested fields and
the long darkness of winters that
guttered speech into stoic silence;
the bones of the first settlers become
another knot in the stubborn tangle of earth.

Some day she knows she will bury her father
where the oiled blade sings neatly
through the green stalks,
and there is so much she wants to hear
from him, so much she would like to have said
before he is lain here like
a length of summer grass.

A father can be as difficult a love
as an adopted country,
how part of him always remains a stranger
how impossible it is to leave cleanly, completely.
        She follows behind him now because
there is nowhere else she can go,
because the summers here are brief,
and as she moves in his shadow
she is thinking about silence, about
the scythe, about the fallen purple lupins
around her feet.

~

Mom's Blues

After the improvised concerto for four children,
after a long solo for unaccompanied kidney stone,
years since her father and brother had been taken
by the tuneless earth
and the song of ash had buried them,
in her fourth decade of carrying
tone-deaf congregations through Presbyterian hymns
in small Newfoundland churches,
my mother has discovered the blues

She listens to it all on late night CBC,
scratchy Mississippi Delta blues on old 78's,
the sting of Chicago blues gone electric,
men keening for a taste of sweet honey and
the women who been done wrong, wrong, wrong —
she loves the call and return
between the singer and the sad guitar,
steel strings bending beneath skin calloused
to the firmness of bone,
and the way the singer's voice breaks
over and over like a heart without
letting go of the song

It's all about longing and loss:
according to the blues, nothing is taken from you
that wouldn't leave of its own accord in the end,
and I think that's what my mother relates to,
the inevitability of it, how even loss can be beautiful
if you need it to be

I imagine her sitting at the church organ
on a staid Sunday morning
with those songs newly settled in her head,
the old Black spirituals crossed
with a naked desire and disappointment
the Presbyterian hymns never touch;
imagine her thinking they haven't changed her so much as
told her what she's known for years now,
that life is a study in the blues afterall,
how sometimes it's sweetest when
it hurts the most

how it hurts so good

~

Sweet Time

I love my apartment on Wellington St
its idiosyncrasies, the crooked wooden
floor, the slow drains, the old pipes that
the bath water comes through
in its own sweet time.
I have never been lonely here:
so many of my friends have warmed
these seats with their bodies,
their mouths kissing the rim of
one of my favourite mugs.
The woman I almost married painted
the green trim in the bedroom, years ago
before I fell in love with her.

Until she saw the place for the first time
my mother said I seemed absent
from my voice when she called,
she had nowhere real to place my body,
no details to set it among
like a vase of flowers on
a lacquered wooden table, near
a curtained window —

The apartment part of what
defines me now, a second skin,
it carries my history like a scar;
when I leave, the green trim will be
passed on to a stranger like a family trait
travelling through generations.

                                        For years
my voice on the telephone will place
me here in my mother's mind,
my face in the light of the floor lamp
beside the stereo.
Some small piece of myself will always
be coming up those stairs from the street
like the water in the pipes, taking
its own sweet time.

~

ONE OF THE LIVES I
HAVE NOT LIVED

— to see everything and to realize the best and worst
of everything
is to love and not forget

Al Purdy

Cigarettes (1)

The day my grandfather died he ate
a meal of salt beef and cabbage in his
sick bed, his appetite returning for
the first time in weeks, the skin
hanging from the bones of his face
like an oversized suit.

My father had gone in to see him
before church that morning, fifteen years old then
and thinking the old man was recovering;
they spoke for a few minutes about the cold
and about going out in the spring,
and then my grandfather asked his son for
a cigarette.

Summers, after the caplin had rolled,
the cod moved into water too deep for the traps
and the two of them would spend the days jigging,
standing at the gunnel with a line down
ten fathoms, repeating the rhythmic full-arm jig
as if they were unsuccessfully trying to
start an engine;
mid-afternoon they'd stop to eat,
stoking the galley's firebox to stew cod's heads
and boil tea, then my grandfather would sit aft
with a pipe, pulling his yellow oilskin jacket
over his head until he was finished.
He'd known for years that my father was smoking
on the sly though he'd never acknowledged it,
hid beneath a coat to give his son
a chance to sneak a cigarette
before they got back to work.

The air in the sick room was so cold
their breath hung in clouds between them.
My grandfather was about to die of cancer or TB
and his son sat beside the bed, his pockets
empty for once of Bugle or Target tobacco,
telling his father he had no cigarette to give him
which happened to be the truth, and felt like
a lie to them both.

~

Morning   Labrador Coast

Morning   Labrador coast
my father is thirteen
no, younger still
eleven maybe twelve
shivering to warm himself in the dark

The rustle of surf behind him
the passiveness of it at this hour
the grumble of men waking early
in the shacks
the steady muffle of piss
smacking a low mound of moss at his feet

He's almost given up on childhood
works a full share on the crew
smokes dried rock-moss rolled in
brown paper out of sight of his father

Each morning he makes fists to work the stiffness
out of his hands and wrists
the skin cracked by sea salt
the joints swollen by sleep after hours of work
he soaks them in the warm salve
of his urine
shakes them dry in the cold air
and turning back to the shacks
he sees stars disappearing in the blue
first light breaking out over the water,
the dories overturned on the grey beach
waiting

~

Cod (1)

Some days the nets came up so full
there was enough cod to swamp the boats
and part of the catch came in with other crews
once they'd filled their own dories to the gunnels,
the silver-grey bodies of the fish rippling
like the surface of a lake
the weight of them around their legs
like stepping thigh-deep into water

Most of the work was splitting and curing
the thin gutting knife slivered up the belly
and everything pulled clear with the sound bone
liver into the oil barrel
the thick tongue cut from the throat
and the splayed fish ready for salting then
set out on a flake to dry

This until one in the morning sometimes
a river of cod across the cutting table
in the yellow swirl of kerosene lamps
and everyone up by three or four
to get back out to the nets with the light

There was no talk of sleep when
the cod were running strong,
a few good weeks could make a season;
if they dreamt at all
in those three brief hours a night
they dreamt of the fish
the cold sweet weight of them,
fin and tail flickering in their heads
like light on the water

~

Cod (2)

August.
      My father has sent the crew
home early for the second year in a row
the cod so scarce he can do
the work himself and still have time
to sit in the evenings
time to think about the flour and molasses
the netting, the coils of rope and twine
the tea and sugar and salt he took
on credit in the spring

Every night he dreams of them plentiful
the size of the fish years ago
big around as your thigh,
the thick shiver of their bodies
coming up in the cod traps

He turned seventeen this February past
his father has been dead two short seasons;
alone at the water's edge he sits
mending a useless net and smoking,
already two hundred dollars in debt
to the merchants

There are no cod in the whole frigging ocean

~

Lilacs

     The well is contaminated and we have to
haul a bucket of water up from the brook;
we pull handfuls of lilacs from the trees
outside the open windows and set them
in glasses through the house to mask the smell
of rooms shut up with themselves for years

     There are old saucers of poison placed
on countertops and mantlepieces, spoor in the pantry
and Dad tells me how he'd chase mice through
the house with a stick when he was a boy
although it was considered bad luck for the fishing
and his father forbid killing them
during the season;
                    in Labrador, he says
you could follow the paths they'd beaten
through the long grass in the dark
but no one raised a hand to them all summer

     There are still two beds in the room
where my father was born in nineteen-thirty
and we roll out our sleeping bags there,
then walk to the corner store for food and beer;
later I watch his face in the pale light
of the coleman lantern
try to connect him to what I know of that time
dust bowl photographs, soup kitchens
stories of vagrants at back doors offering
to chop wood for a meal
but I know I have it hopelessly wrong —
he wanted nothing more for me
than that I should grow up a stranger to all this
that his be one of the lives I have not lived

After the lights are put out
there is a silence broken only by the sounds
we make as we shift in our beds and
the occasional scuffle of mice in the hallway;
the age of the house gives a musty
undertone to the sweet smell of the lilacs
and it seems stronger in the darkness
so that I imagine I am breathing in what's left
of the world my father knew
while the part of him that has never
managed to leave here is asleep across the room

~

Life in the Old House

H.M.C.

When he came back to live
at the old house he slept
on a daybed in the kitchen,
divorced from the world,
living mostly on toast and
whiskey mixed with well water
even after oil leeched underground,
the residue rainbowed across
the drink's surface,
the taste in his mouth that
he couldn't spit out.
He had his pension check,
a veteran's allowance,
a box of old photographs
he rarely looked at:
himself in uniform before heading overseas,
his first wife, their two infant children.

The windows sieved by winter wind
he lay beside the stove
half drunk in the light of a bare bulb,
ignoring a hockey game on the radio;
once a week he ate next door,
speaking only to curse the weather
or the metric system,
leaving after dark with leftovers
wrapped in tinfoil,
a nod to Annie in her window
watching him go.

The old house abandoned again now,
though the radio is still there,
the daybed beside the stove.
The box of photos
in a dresser drawer upstairs,
silouhette of a life left behind
by the one who lived it,
faint but unmistakeable,
like the lingering taste of oil
in an old man's mouth.

~

Ski Hill

On a clear day you could see the entire town from there,
the rows of company houses and backyard fences,
the Union Hall, the community pool,
the cottage hospital where my mother worked
off and on for fifteen years;
three church spires, two small schools,
the ballfield where my father slipped and broke his leg
in a rundown between third and home before I was born

Down the hill's back slope the grey remains of a wooden ski run
closed long before my parents married
by lack of snow and the cost of keeping it running,
unrecognizable as anything now but the scar of something human
almost buried in shrubs and moss and blueberry bushes
and beyond that the worthless sprawling beauty
of the barrens

The scrawl of mills to the south-east
smokey-grey buildings stained yellow with sulphur,
around them the train sheds and core-shacks
the huge red warehouse where they laid ice
every winter before the arena was built
and housed almost the entire population on Saturday nights
when the Corner Brook Royals came to town

The white staff office out front, a sign proclaiming
ASARCO: TRESPASSERS WILL BE PROSECUTED;
the double line of railway tracks that marked
the border of company property
where strikers stood every four years
with placards and cigarettes, occasionally
burning a train caboose to the wheels
upending a management car that had
tried to cross the picket line

Out of sight behind the mills are the Glory Holes
excavations the size of small lakes,
and underneath it all the tangle of shafts
where men worked eight hours a shift
drilling the darkness for zinc and copper,
eating a daily sandwich lunch

My mother watched them come in at regular intervals
cursing ugly cuts or sprains
or just the pain   the goddamn pain
of a limb suddenly missing or maimed
by their machines or blind rock or a long fall in the dark
And once every three years or so,
a man she would know by name
wheeled in beneath the white silence of a sheet

At the far edge of town the three grave-yards placed side by side
a triptych of fenced cemeteries,
most of the plots overgrown now
with shrubs and weeds grazing high as the rowed headstones,
tree roots cracking rectangles of concrete
Homes standing empty, doorways and window frames
turning grey with the weather,
a few people left to small pensions and welfare
and to memories like these,
the scar of something human that's had its season
something I've never known as intimately
or seen as clear as I did those early summer afternoons
watching it from the bare skull of Ski Hill

~

Cigarettes (2)

When my father gave up smoking
the thing he found hardest was knowing
what to do with his hands
the first fifteen minutes after a meal,
and driving into town is like that now —
what you notice first are the things that are
no longer here
the double row of bunkhouses torn down
the green clapboard mess hall
the old storage shed behind the pool
that had once been a stable for
the company horses
long before the road went through

After supper Dad and I take a swing
onto company property, circle in behind
the fenced crater of the Glory Hole where
                          almost everything is missing
the deck heads at Rothemere and MacLean's
felled like trees
core shacks and warehouses bulldozed
the concrete stumps of the shower rooms
left naked in the ground where they were poured
                          fifty years ago

Only the mill is still on its feet
ash-coloured, useless
waiting to be taken down like an old photograph
and turned to the wall in an attic room

Thirty years   my father says, turning slowly
and I remember a story about a horse he drove
when he came here to work in '47
the mare nuzzling his shirt pocket for tobacco
first thing in the mornings
snatching hand-rolled cigarettes straight
from his lips if he tried to light up
in front of her
                Gone now, sold off by the company
and dead somewhere
Molly, I think her name was

Still, I have only a vague idea of what's been lost;
my father is surrounded by more than
the simple absence I can see here
                a life he's not quite finished with going on
just beyond what he's able to touch
like the impossible ache of a phantom limb
or that craving, the automatic fumbling for
the cigarette pack he's forgotten is
no longer there

~

South of Badger

South of Badger the forest stutters effortlessly
over low rolling hills
long stretches of birch and alder
the darkness of spruce trees crowding the road

My people came this way by river from the coast
Englishmen carrying rifles, trinkets, small pox,
a distrust of the unnamed
they stumbled on a habitat for nomads
for hunters and gatherers
the barrens opening onto acres of shrub land
brush land, miles of moss covered rock
where nothing has ever grown by design
bog land, breeding ground for water fowl and insects,
                              for pitcher plants
deep fresh water lakes home to the crooked snouts
of salmon and nine pound trout

Somewhere in there they found a pocket of ore
laced with veins of copper, zinc
a little gold and silver
they traded all they had brought but the rifles
constructed a town over shrub land, brush land
building houses, schools, a hockey rink
and eighty miles of dead-end highway
men burrowing thousands of feet into earth to harvest dust
busted rock winched out of darkness for seventy-odd years
till the mine was defeated by the country's stinginess
and the company shut it down

Coming up that road for the first time in years
through Buchans Jct. in the dark and driving slow
half-a-dozen times the headlights answered by
the dumb stare of moose happy to be free
of forest underbrush
they can't believe their luck
to have stumbled on a clear path north
and there's not enough traffic these days
to give it much human meaning;
they relinquish it with some reluctance
looking back as they lope into the near trees
the car passing by on the temporary pavement,
already the forest is working to bury what's
been left behind

~

PART OF IT

Don't speak to me about
politics. I've got eyes, man.

Sharon Olds

Bullet

This poem
for the bullet that killed Romero

because it was
silver and inevitable

because it had
a head like a nail

because it carried a message from
someone wealthy and frightened and desperate

because it had a dark sort of grace
when it sang into the heart of the priest
like a choir,
like a slender tongue of flame

because it laid him out at the altar
like a jilted lover

because it lodged there
in the painful pulse of blood
as if it could be anonymous

the bullet that killed Romero
thinking *Well*
that's finished it.

~

What They Are Fighting For

The ones who did not fight
who marched peacefully in the streets
and were shot by soldiers placed
strategically on the roofs
around the square;
                or were photographed there
added to a file, a list of names
and were taken from their beds at night
their tongues gouged from their mouths,
the skin peeled from their faces
and hung in a tree

Their history, the generations warped
and broken on the plantations
like so many sticks of lumber,
the slow smoulder of sickness and hunger
in the bones of their parents
and their parents' parents

It is not an end to poverty they kill for
but an end to wealth,
the obscenity of it

They live in the hills, carry their lives
and their lives only on their backs;
sleep under trees where the faces
of those they fight for look
down at them, silently
without hope or fear

~

The Deaths of Oscar Romero

His vestments behind glass
the blood dried brown
the purple cloth stained a deeper purple
from a single bullet's mess

If they kill me   he said
I will arise again in the Salvadoran people

In the countryside they squat in
bombed out haciendas
they live in shanty towns on the outskirts
of the city, in tin and cardboard houses
there is no work, no food for days at a time
the most outspoken are assassinated

The Monsignor dies every day in El Salvador
they have cut his tongue from
a thousand different mouths

~

Witness

The soldiers came into our village in
broad daylight as calm as saints of God
and started killing.
I saw my 13 year old daughter fall and
a bullet passed through my forearm
as I ran by her corpse, following the others
into the jungle where we hid under leaves,
our hands over the mouths of the children
to keep them from crying out.
The soldiers chased us to the edge
of the village and fired blindly into
the foliage where we lay,
the trees splintering above our heads
and I was praying the whole time,
I wanted to be praying when they killed me.

After the shooting stopped
they gathered the bodies into a pile,
doused them with gasoline and burned them,
then they set fire to our homes,
standing in the red light of the flames
as the sun went down.
And we were watching from the jungle behind them,
the silhouette of soldiers between us
and our burning homes and night
falling everywhere.

~

Part of It

for J.C.

I was in love with you all that week in El Salvador
in fact I think all of us were in love with you some,
made up our little fantasies about staying behind
to live with you and a dream of justice
                    or maybe that's just romanticizing
and it was only sleeping with you
we were interested in;
but it wasn't just because you were young and beautiful
and naively idealistic, not just because
you were grateful to us for being there.
It was the entire country we had the hots for,
that ridiculous hope we wanted to be
                              part of somehow —
it was you more than anyone who showed us
Salvador naked and real, so it was you we wanted
Jennifer.

It's been a week now since government troops
buried rifles in your backyard and
dug them up for the cameras,
arresting you as a rebel supporter.
I don't have any illusions about what that means for you.
Part of this poem is an apology for being able
to say these things, for living in comfortable
conservative Kingston Ontario Canada
where all we have to fear are accidents, blind fate;
part of it is to ask forgiveness for writing
what amounts to romantic crap about you and Salvador
when all I'm after is probably just another
publication credit in a small, respected
Canadian literary journal.

Some people have tried to justify this kind
of exploitation in the name of art
but to me that's just rhetoric,
propaganda I can't bring myself to believe in.
There are no excuses for the way we live our lives,
there isn't even ignorance to cover our heads
with anymore.
                    I know you are being tortured in
a Salvadoran prison; I know you have been
raped there, and not just because you are
young and beautiful

and this poem is part of that too
somehow

November, 1989

~

Structural Adjustment:
An Introduction

Crops grown for export:

Coffee, soybeans, the long leafless sticks
of sugar cane like a harvest of alders,
field after field of cotton where
pickers stoop and bob in the heat.
Tropical fruit.
                     Mangoes, papayas,
the dark skull of coconuts, bananas
peaches, comical pineapple heads
their green shocks of hair standing
straight up.
                Thick congregations of
grapes growing heavy with sunlight.

For local consumption:

Mostly beans and rice, corn, sometimes
a little squash on small plots of land,
sometimes nothing.
                  Chronic malnutrition
infant mortality, field after field of
political rhetoric, riots, sanctioned repression.
Rifles imported from the old Soviet Union
or from America, it hardly matters which.

~

Structural Adjustment:
The IMF Representative's Advice

The way we see it, your first priority is to repay your foreign creditors. There is no other way to see it. If we may be candid in this discussion, you have nothing to offer investors but cheap labour and raw resources, as does everyone in your position. So.

Forget corporate taxes, they are the leprosy of international trade, no one will come near you. The country's currency will be devalued to make goods and services more cheaply available to everyone but your own people. And if we may speak off the record, we suggest that you discourage unions, they are never happy, they cause trouble for everyone. Let me put it this way: *strongly* discourage unions. I hope we understand one another on this point. And we will require fiscal restraint in the form of less domestic spending, an end to food subsidies and your program to subsidize the cost of milk for infants which our balance sheets clearly indicate you cannot afford.

You will excuse me for speaking so bluntly. There are many people with an interest in helping you make your payments and we are here to assist in any way we can. If you refuse to cooperate we will choke you the way weeds choke a garden of flowers.

~

Atrocities

Don't bore me with your talk
about atrocities.
      Your poems.
There are people who see the human body
as a receptacle for pain, every inch of flesh
flowers with possibilities for them,
an ear a finger a nipple
they're as imaginative as lovers.
This isn't news.
        People want the details
so they can be sickened and outraged
so they can feel as if they have reacted,
done something.

Try telling them about economics
say something about *transnationals*, the World Bank
about *structural adjustment*.
        Ask them who pays
the torturer, who profits when he touches
a body so skilfully that every nerve
quivers like a lit filament and the bowels
empty into the victim's pants.
Ask them who pays.
      Don't bore me with your talk
they'll say.

~

Victor Jara's Hands

The aim is to take the best of what
these people are, Victor Jara's hands
stolen from his wrists to silence his music
his guitar like an amputated limb
sitting dumb and useless in a corner;
Romero assassinated in a chapel
as he raised the chalice toward heaven,
as if God were being implicated:
your faith is useless
the killers wanted to say

Thousands of others, the anonymous ones
who refuse to shut their mouths
and end up in cells lined with shag carpet
where they are taught to be silent,
slowly

                  Sometimes entire villages
buried together in unmarked graves
buildings levelled, as if memory itself
could be bulldozed, turned under soil
crops charred in the fields,
so much suffering you'd think
nothing would ever grow from the ground again

But something remains, something remains
and will not die
though it is killed over and over:

from the scorched earth
something rises and has its say,
a woman's calloused voice,
a pair of hands finding a guitar
and playing it until the fingers bleed.

~

REDEFINING
THE KISS

we are joined in the ideological cuddle

Billy Bragg

Come to me
with the kiss
re-defined . . .

Brenda Brooks

Reading Ondaatje

The way you imagine he'd like
to be read —
     2am, a bed near the floor,
a single lamp spilling its mane of yellow
light across the varnished hardwood,
the beige sheets

You move your fingers through
the woman's hair as she reads aloud
from a soft cover copy of
In the Skin of a Lion —
she's telling a stranger's story
as if it could be her own,
moving through unfamiliar rooms
with blind assurance, her voice
a filament of light drawing words from
the darkness outside the lamp's circle,
her slight lisp like a fingerprint
on every syllable

After each section she pauses
and you are suddenly aware of
her body beside you, the heat
where your limbs lie on her skin;
she can taste herself on your mouth,
the fanned pages of the book
close slowly in her hand
like an animal settling into sleep —

     When she turns back to the novel
your hand is beneath her hair
cupping the private curve of the ear
eyes closed to follow the story,
your lips just touching her shoulder,
the nearly translucent skin

～

Redefining The Kiss: Women

Loving women is like sitting in
on a conversation between beautiful strangers,
their words full of polite platonic affection
like a kiss between relatives;
I can spend hours talking with them
or listening as they speak among themselves,
wondering what it is they'd be saying
if I wasn't around

I enjoy being close to women,
I admire their honesty about love
and their incongruous optimism,
their willingness to trust even
those things I distrust in myself —

Sometimes I think a woman's body is
the only distance between a man and a woman,
sometimes it's that distance I'm in love with

Some of the women I've loved have
fallen in love with
other women
                it's strange to see them
in the light of their new partners,
knowing something of
how they like to be touched —
like a memory of a past life,
my body grazed by a world
it has no claim to,
and I don't have the words to say
how beautiful, how far beyond me
they are

They look so happy I could
just kiss them

~

Redefining The Kiss: Men

Loving men is like listening to a song
on the radio
       you can stand beside it and sing along
but it's hard to get any closer

A man's body is the distance
he puts between himself and other men,
and it's a distance he's in love with

When two men sleep together they are
careful not to touch, even accidentally,
as if an electric current between them could singe
their skin, fill the room with the stink of burnt hair

Men greet each other with slaps and punches,
otherwise they're as prim as a handshake
on a first date

Someone offering you a mouthful
of their beer is the closest you'll
ever come to a kiss

~

Deborah, Praying

I am imagining this.
Except the room, I have seen the room.
There is a bed. A desk.
There are flowers.
There is a bible on the nightstand
beside the bed.
It has an imitation leather cover
and in the Gospels the words of Christ
are set out in red type.
I have always considered this tacky
but I don't think so anymore.

She is sitting on the edge of the bed
with the bible in her lap.
The reading lamp is on
but she is not reading now.
Her eyes are closed
her hair has fallen across her face;
one hand is curled into a loose fist
at her mouth and her lips
move slightly behind it.
I am listening closely, but I can't
make out the words and I think
I'm relieved I can't
make out the words.
She is praying.

I am praying too.

~

Salt

Like to say I've known love and hate,
to say I've risen above it all,
keeper of the Buddha's detachment,
his enlightened perspective on
the different forms our selfishness takes

Sarah left a container of sea salt
over the stove when we split up
and I don't know what keeps it there,
why I don't give it back or throw it out,
nostalgia or pettiness, it's hard to say

The Buddha could have made a parable of it,
how the salt crystallizes like
an enlightened consciousness when
the water in which it's dispersed evaporates,
the wisdom of the smallest things opening
to him like a lover's mouth

It's hard to believe the stories
of his adolescence, to think that back
when he was a lascivious prince
he might have had a thing for Sarah too,
to hell with the salt and what it could mean;
I have so far to go that sometimes the distance
seems impossible, but there is some
small consolation in that

~

David Donnell's Schlong

I've got fairly interesting genitals myself

What Men Have Instead of Skirts

He wants you to think he's being ironic
and playful when his dick comes up in the poems
inevitable as a prairie sunrise
and the women who can't resist it
the ones he revolves between like homes in
the city and the country outside Toronto
writing lyrics about their delicate raspberry tongues
on the double-cheese-and-bacon-hot-pepper pizza of
     his cock;
even when it isn't mentioned his penis stirs
beneath the poems restless as an insomniac
bulging under the lines like a tent pole —
the young potato pickers hefting their skirts and
fucking under fences in the fields
the women gleaming with gold dust and sweat
who dance naked on the backs of horses(!) —
his horses are always alter egos for his libido
for his magnificent rod standing wet and erect
swollen to the size of a tree.

All the while he contemplates his immigrant vision
of America or his sleek liver-coloured hound
or Louis Satchmo Armstrong dimpling his trumpet
under cover afterhours you can feel
the silent one-eyed stare of that leafless stalk
that pink stick of celery demanding attention,
he wants you to think it's satire
that it's self-depreciating humour and maybe
he thinks this himself as he writes his poems about
rutabagas and Emily Dickinson and the sad sewer fate
     of semen

but the poems don't believe it
they aren't distracted by references to dead uncles
and histories of the Canadian National Railway
and they don't always believe he believes it either
those cocky grazers in the sweet grass of
his cities and old provincial towns
those elastic exquisite right hands   those elegant
        dark flowers.

~

Precedents: A Meditation on The Bobbitts

The setting: night, a slight breeze
a sickle moon

A car pulls off onto a shoulder of highway
and something is thrown from
the window by a woman's hand,
a delicate dark hand that is
tapered like a feather

The something lands among dust and
blades of grass,
lies motionless but poised somehow
a curl of flesh like a swan's neck
folded neatly into a nest of green

Take a moment to reflect on these things,
on the precedents

               There is the Native legend of
the penis that sprouts wings, simple bird
of prey, slipping through the teepee's smoke hole
after the fire has cooled into darkness,
finding its way to the naked lap
of a girl while her family snores around her,
the boy waiting nearby, watching the sky
for its return

Beside the highway our curl of flesh
lies incomplete, an apostrophe
abandoned by all the old familiar stories
too timid and forlorn to become
the evening's exclamation mark

Somewhere a boy is watching the dark horizon,
cursing, convinced that something has been
stolen from him —
                    before long he will come by here
looking for what has been lost

~

Michelangelo

After the argument the woman lies there
knees up, her back straight against
the hardwood floor;
she wants to be perfectly still, wants
her heart to stop beating for a moment,
she is reaching for the smooth
colourless patience of marble
of stone

The man in the chair beside her won't shut up,
chisels the air around her with words,
with small unintentional cruelties,
he diminishes her with
the mindlessness of time

She thinks of a picture she's seen
of the Sistine Chapel in Rome,
remembers a story about Michelangelo
lying like this for months on a scaffold,
his face inches from the sky
the stillness of the hand held aloft, painting
recalling the way a life begins,
a world

She wants to understand the process
what it's like to be up there;
she wants to lie perfectly still
to start all over again
smooth and faceless as the ceiling

If she looks at the man
she will fall

~

Redefining The Kiss: Wanda's Dream

She is looking for a new apartment
and we are standing alone in an unfurnished room;
our voices echo slightly in the naked space,
the walls stripped of decoration
and the dream's atmosphere is charged by
this vacancy, the room empty of everything
but potential.
Wanda begins kissing me, her wet tongue
in my mouth as she touches me here,
and here, and here, and then
she sends me off to look for a condom.
She removes her skirt, her underwear,
and discovers she has an erect penis;
she is surprised but unperturbed by this,
proceeds to unwrap the condom I have found
and roll the sheath clumsily
along the length of the cock,
feeling as if she is trying to tie someone else's shoelaces
or read a message reflected in a mirror.
I can do this, she coaches herself, *I've done this before.*

In the dream, I am not disturbed
by this turn of events either.
I am still fully clothed and
Wanda has no idea whether I have
male or female genitalia,
but she assumes we can work it out.
The walls around us are white and bare
waiting to be hung with Wanda's photos,
her Group of Seven prints,
but in the dream she is thinking
she might like to leave them as they are.

Once she has dealt with the condom
she kisses me again
her tongue attentive as a bee at a flower
and in the few moments before she wakes
she feels as if almost anything
could happen.

~

Undomestic

Late November, late afternoon,
how the light fails like everything
I thought I knew about loving a woman.
Strips of moose meat from the fall hunt
on paper towels beside the stove,
speckled with salt and pepper,
bacon grease heating in a skillet.
The dog staring up at the smell of blood.
Before she lifts them to the pan
Wanda cuts a morsel of raw flesh
from a steak and places it in
her mouth, chewing slowly as she cooks.
The line of muscle working in her cheeks,
the look on my face she doesn't see.
The dog whining and shifting on
his haunches.

After the dishes are cleared away
a light snow begins falling outside;
there's a hockey game on the radio,
the rasp of skates creasing ice
barely audible beneath the announcer's voice.
The dog is asleep beside the fire and growling,
dreaming something undomestic.
Wanda's face almost the face of a stranger
in the light of the kerosene lamp
as she lifts me above and inside her,
as I taste the salt on her lips, her mouth,
believing I can learn to love
everything about her that I still
do not know.

~

Almost Everything

Turn a flat stone in a garden:
the scramble of ants in new light,
columns of purposeful motion
or handfuls scattered in a blind pattern

I want to be that busy
beneath your body
that engaged
to know you above me as
darkness, shelter

Gandhi once claimed that almost
everything we do in life
is meaningless
                but it is essential
that we do what
life presents to us

I want to touch you as if
that were true
with the same sense
of inevitability and peace
                to kiss you
because I'm convinced
that it's necessary
though I could not give you
a single reason why

~

THE RIVER
YOU REMEMBER

. . . all I know is what I am
and even this I don't fully understand.

Carolyn Smart

Only strangers travel.

Leonard Cohen

Silk Road (1)

*. . .the foreignness of what you no longer are
or no longer possess awaits you in foreign,
unpossessed places.*

Italo Calvino

Where the Silk Road begins,
Xi'an
        from here through the Gobi desert
and Pakistan
and on as far as Europe

At the top of the Big Wild Goose Pagoda
a view of the city and my stomach
turning, wanting out of the open air
wanting the comfort of stairs and walls
though I'm not usually afraid of heights

Perhaps I fell from here
in another lifetime
in sight of the old city wall,
jumped maybe, an unhappy lover
or was pushed
a gambler in debt to the wrong people

Nothing's more improbable than being here at all,
my body reliving an event
that my mind no longer recalls,
anticipating a kind of absence
that first step into air like
the panic of forgetting your own name
your address
the faces of people you love

Where the journey begins is
there
           that fall into a part of myself
I was past remembering

~

In Canada There Is Already Snow

At six each morning
there is a Tai Chi lesson
beside the teacher's dorm.
She wears loose clothing,
stretch pants, a sweat shirt
her roommate's red tam
to keep her ears warm.
In a month it will be
too cold to practice outside.

After breakfast there are classes
two dozen voices chanting
awkward North American "good mornings,"
the students stumbling eagerly
through a foreign language
that she lays out like
an obstacle course in front of them.

Most afternoons are free,
she travels downtown to the post office
on a bike provided by the school,
her bare fingers turning
red as the country's flag
on the handlebars.

Twice a week there is a letter
from a man in Canada
where there is already snow.
She trades the stamps wordlessly
with the old men who hang out there,
pointing, shaking her head
yes or no.

At dinner she argues with her roommate
about everything
they love each other with
the fierceness of lost strangers.
By nine the sun is gone,
she has written a letter,
prepared tomorrow's lesson.

There are one hundred and fifty-four
matches in the drawer
beside her bed.
Each night she lights one more,
falls asleep in the flash
of darkness that follows.

~

Forge

Halfway to the school there's a group
of blacksmiths working at small portable forges
along the roadside, hammering iron bodies
around the words in their mouths,
a coal shovel almost there on the anvil
two men struggling with its red-hot syllable
like stubborn lexicographers,
their alternating hammer strokes
demanding *what do you mean?*
what do you mean goddamn it?
while the sun beats across their backs

A toddler wearing crotchless pants
stops to piss in the street nearby
and there's something disarmingly true
about his simple squat in the middle
of bicycle traffic,
his head shaved bald as a Buddhist monk's,
the unconcerned look of meditation
on his face as he urinates
      and I can't help connecting the two
in this afternoon heat,
the boy finishing up now and straightening
as if from prayer,
the smiths behind him slamming
their metal tongues against
unrepentant shapelessness,
parts of a whole the poem includes,
is included in, but I can't quite get it,
squinting against the difficult sunlight,
and no one else seems to notice a thing —

young Buddha wanders off in search of a parent,
the two men break for a cigarette and some conversation
and maybe there was nothing there
at all —

Hefei, Anhui Province
China

~

Insomniac Trains

Insomniac trains steam
all the unforgiving night across
the north China wilderness,
their wakefulness a kind of hunger
a kind of desperation;
they rail through oceans of dense heat,
howl on the outskirts of sleeping cities
like Old Testament prophets,
their dark calls going unheeded

Stare out the window at 4am
hollow with sleeplessness,
the insomniac train rocking through desert
and a wordless moon travelling above you,
a vowel sound, a silver hum in the night sky
Two days from now you'll watch
a man die on the sidewalk
beside a railway station,
a beer-bellied housefly circling
the brown quarter of his left nipple,
pulse shuddering to a stop like an old freight,
the half-closed eyes as speechless
as the moon

It's a slow process
he's lying there already tonight
unconscious and falling into a darkness
that is deeper than the darkness
you are travelling through,
the insomniac train ticking
you towards him on the rails,
a relentless eye of light in the desert,
an open mouth that swallows and swallows
three bright metres of track

~

News from Home: Winter

Frost laces the window
with white,
winter's elegant geometry.
             Fingernail traces
a crystal line,
ice crawling down the spine
like panic;
my mother's voice on the telephone,
words falling like intricate
stars of snow,
       spelling out
another human accident in
the green mathematics
of a Labrador forest.

Lost for days probably,
       trudging through the
emptiness of winter
reciting the alphabet
the sanity of the 9X tables
            till the frost
bleached his mind clean
till he lay beneath the innocent trees,
his mouth a frozen blue vowel
his eyes sewn shut by
the sharp thread of the cold.

~

The Bath

She's working at a camp on the Rwandan border,
speaking broken French to refugees —
her freckled skin, a stethescope,
the thick braid of a ponytail
over her shoulder.
   Remember her taking a bath
at my apartment one afternoon
in August before she finished school,
how she pulled the damp hair back
with a band,
its wet length marking her dress
almost to the waist.

A young girl is carried in on a stretcher
unconscious and dying of meningitis,
her father tells them the headache
began yesterday, the fever overnight;
the canvas tent lends a stale yellow sheen
to the light inside,
Leslie's white shirt looks beige,
her light brown hair is almost
the colour of straw.
She sits beside the girl
listening to the healthy helpless
lunge of the heart
and I suppose she's forgotten
that afternoon in Kingston,
the bath, and Sharon cutting her bangs
on the fire escape afterwards —
I remember the sound of
their voices outside,
the careful snip of the scissors
like footsteps over gravel.

The father is sitting at the head
of the stretcher, confused by
his daughter's sudden illness and
the white doctor's language,
by the translator telling him
there is nothing they can do;
distracted, he doesn't notice when
the girl stops breathing and
her heart slows, then stops as well.
Fini, Leslie tells him
and he turns toward her, startled,
like a man who has fallen asleep
at a theatre and wakes to find
the movie has ended.
She has to repeat herself
                    Fini, she says.

Leslie, I remember it was August
and Sharon had carried a chair out
onto the fire escape,
your hair still wet from the bath.

You were wearing a green dress.

~

Rivers/Roads

I thought I was following a track of freedom
and for awhile it was

Adrienne Rich

Consider the earnestness of pavement
its dark elegant sheen after rain,
its insistence on leading you somewhere

A highway wants to own the landscape,
it sections prairie into neat squares
swallows mile after mile of countryside
to connect the dots of cities and towns,
to make sense of things

A river is less opinionated
less predictable
it never argues with gravity
its history is a series of delicate negotiations with
geography and time

Wet your feet all you want
Hericlitus says,
it's never the river you remember;
a road repeats itself incessantly
obsessed with its own small truth,
it wants you to believe in something particular

The destination you have in mind when you set out
is nowhere you have ever been;
where you arrive finally depends on
how you get there,
by river or by road

~

Small Animals

Little traffic between Sharbot Lake
and Kingston, late night Sunday
the quiet highway does its best
to keep me awake —
road signs flare up like
tall matches: speed limits
official proclamations on litter
and population
sudden moments of colour I no longer
try to read or comprehend.

      The eyes of small animals
spark red along the roadside
and go out in the darkness.

We drive through entire towns
asleep and unaware of us
                only the occasional gold tooth
of a porch light waiting up
for someone arriving late.

And Sarah's sleeping too beside me
her head against the darkness
of the window;
I catch quick glimpses of her face
its small surprising beauty.

There's a word for this
           I've almost found
a word that explains us
I can almost speak out loud.
When she wakes up I want to say it
tell her we're closer now
to perfection
than we've ever been.

The headlights push their pale
fingers along the pavement
the road moving beneath them
          like a long flawless story.

Over and over a word sparks
red in my mouth

stutters out in darkness.

~

Silk Road (2)

Everything is in motion,
even what is still.

Robert Bly

Train rocks north and west
through dark countryside toward Xinjiang
soft lights in the windows and open doorways
of houses along the tracks
occasional shifting of sleepers behind me
coughing
bits of conversation made intimate by the darkness

Driving home from Grand Falls
years ago
        my brothers asleep beside me
in the back seat
a low moon following through trees
on the Buchans highway,
already I have so much to remember

Dawn there now, the highway deserted

Everything I have ever been
sits motionless
at the open window of the train,
doorways silhouette the bodies of strangers

Darkness, the small light
of other lives

~

The Road Home

I think the land knows we are here,
I think the land knows we are strangers.

Al Purdy

The highway takes you only so far,
roadsigns and pavement right to the coast of
the mainland and the island somewhere out
there beyond it, a rock cradled in fog,
a gloved fist

The ferry shoulders its way into the north Atlantic,
into rain and an easterly wind, making for
Newfoundland which is no longer my home
but the place I come from still
the place that made me
and being a stranger there now I am
more or less a stranger wherever I find myself

From the terminal in Port Aux Basques
the TransCanada works north up the coast,
picking its way through the Long Range mountains
before turning east to the interior of
spruce forests and marsh, clouds of black flies,
acres of rolling barrens
where only wind and rain and winter have
ever been completely at home;
driving through, I recognize the landscape
but not my place in it, a stiff wind
rocks the car like a small boat,
and I don't have the words to say
the countryside properly though I feel it
moving inside me, its dark strength

Coming home teaches me that I own nothing,
that there is nothing in the world
I have a claim to
though this one place has a claim to me —
turning south onto the Buchans highway
I follow the Exploits River further into bush,
through Buchans Jct. buried in waves of spruce
and past the cold length of Red Indian Lake which has
forgotten me completely since I left
here years ago . . .

~

Notes On The Poems

Bullet

Oscar Romero, Archbishop of San Salvador, was assassinated in March 1980 because of his outspoken criticism of economic injustice and human rights abuses by the military, government, and right wing "death squads".

The Deaths of Oscar Romero

Despite the end of the civil war in El Salvador, the extreme poverty which created the conflict has actually worsened in the last twelve years. Human rights abuses have been significantly curbed since the signing of the Peace Accords in 1992, but "death squads" are still active and the threat of abductions and extra-judicial executions of people involved in opposition political parties, labour unions, women's, church, and human rights groups is a daily reality.

Witness

The poem is based on eye-witness accounts of the "Scorched Earth" policy adopted by the Guatemalan military in the early 1980s. In the space of four years more than 400 indigenous communities were destroyed, thousands of Mayans were assassinated, and approximately 100,000 survived by escaping across the border into Mexico.

Structural Adjustment: An Introduction and The IMF Representative's Advice

Structural Adjustment is a program imposed by the International Monetary Fund and the World Bank on countries unable to make payments on their national debt. It includes forcing countries to gear production toward exports to bring in cash, ending "protectionist" measures to allow an influx of foreign business and capital, as well as slashing spending on social programs (sound familiar anyone?). All of which keeps the money flowing into northern banks and financial institutions while millions of people do not have access to enough food, or medical treatment, or education.

Under Structural Adjustment, the IMF also oversees and approves a country's budgeting and finance, with unofficial but effective veto power over almost all aspects of a country's affairs.

David Donnell's Schlong

Number of poems in DD's Governor General's Award Winning collection *Settlements*: 70

Number which feature an appearance by, or reference to, the poet's or another man's penis: 12

Number of references to the male genitalia (cock, schlong, balls, erection, etc) in "Driving in From Muskoka Slow Rain Blues": 9

Number of poems which include a reference to or description of sex (fucking, making love, entering from behind, etc): 21

Not counting the above, the number in which appearances are made by a naked woman, a woman in her underwear, a woman cupping her naked breasts, a woman seductively shaking her hips, pulling her skirt up to her waist or ripping her dress, etc: 17

Number in which a piece of red pepper is picked off the poet's erect penis by a woman's delicate raspberry tongue: 1

Number in which beautiful women gleaming with gold dust and sweat dance naked on the backs of horses: 1

Number in which silent horses masturbate compulsively: 1

Number in which bears pant with lust: 1

Number in which the poet admits an insatiable desire to produce a thousand erections: 1

Precedents: A Meditation on the Bobbitts

From the "How Quickly We Forget" File. Lorena Bobbitt cut off her husband's penis while he was sleeping; after leaving the house with the severed organ, she threw it from her car window into a field. According to Lorena, the emasculation was in retaliation for the physical and emotional abuse she had suffered at the hands of John Wayne Bobbitt during their marriage.

The penis was eventually located and reattached. Both of the Bobbitts were cleared of charges in separate trials. John Wayne Bobbitt has since gone on to make at least one pornographic movie.

Acknowledgements

Many of these poems have appeared previously or have been accepted for publication, sometimes in different form, in the following magazines and anthologies: *Breathing Fire: Canada's New Poets* (Harbour Publishing); *Wild on the Crest* (Jeroboam Books); *More Garden Varieties Two* (Mercury/Aya Press); *The Antigonish Review, Arc, The Capilano Review, The Dalhousie Review, Dandelion, Event, The Fiddlehead, Grain, The Malahat Review, The New Quarterly, Poetry Canada, Prairie Fire, Vintage 96* (Quarry Press), *Prism international, Quarry* and *TickleAce*.

A number have been broadcast on CBC Stereo's *The Arts Tonight*, and on CBC St. John's *Weekend Arts Magazine* and *The Fisheries Broadcast*. Others were featured on *The Writer's Project* on CFRC Queen's University Radio.

I Owe You A Beer . . .

Wanda, for the space to write and for the cats; my parents, for letting me have my way with their lives; my brothers Paul, Stephen and Peter, for saving for my retirement; Amber, for loving the printed word; the Thursday night Brew, Cue and You Gang: w & a, Marney, Brenda, Andrea, Helen, JackieFast, and guest members; Pam and Mike for a bed in *Town*; Ignacio Melgar, for not letting me forget; Carolyn Smart, for constant encouragement and support; Nancy Kroeker and others at the Writer's Development Trust, ditto; Don Maynard for permission to use "Leaving the Farm" on the cover; Shari-Shari for the "yawning dog" photograph; Sarah, for the tux. Everyone who took the time to read and comment on poems in this collection (all of the above, and Ann Montgomery, Jan McAlpine, Megan Williams, Steve Heighton, Patrick Lane, Lorna Crozier, Marlene Cookshaw, Derk Wynand, Jake Klisivitch).